THE OFFIC

England Rugby

ANNUAL 2020

Written by **Michael Rowe**

Designed by **Daniel May**

A Grange Publication

ISBN 978-1-913034-36-8

CONTENTS

WELCOME
England Rugby fans!

Rugby is the best sport in the world, and there has never been a better time to be an England Rugby fan.

All over the country millions of young (and old!) people enjoy rugby every week. They have great fun, make new friends and keep themselves fit. This book is a celebration of everything that you love about England Rugby.

You'll find the inside line on your favourite players, reports on big matches and lots of fun activities as well.

We are sure you will enjoy this book. Let's cheer the England Rugby teams towards another great year of success!

Swing Low!

England Six Nations Fixtures 2020

Sunday 2nd February 2020
France v England
Stade de France, 15:00

Saturday 8th February 2020
Scotland v England
BT Murrayfield, 16:45

Sunday 23rd February 2020
England v Ireland
Twickenham, 15:00

Saturday 7th March 2020
England v Wales
Twickenham, 16:45

Saturday 14th March 2020
Italy v England
Stadio Olimpico, 16:45

All times are UK times (GMT/BST).

SIX NATIONS

WHAT A COMEBACK!

Ireland 20–32 England
Aviva Stadium • 2nd February 2019

England simply blew Ireland away, giving possibly their best ever performance under Eddie Jones.

Ireland had won the 2018 title, and Grand Slam, with a convincing win at Twickenham – leaving England to finish in disappointing fifth place.

There was to be no repeat. A sizzling start from the men in white saw a try after one minute. Manu Tuilagi was straight into the action, bursting onto a long throw from Jamie George and making ground upfield. Several drives later, Owen Farrell gave a truly epic pass and Jonny May was over in the corner. Brilliant!

England were superb all over the pitch, Mako Vunipola being made Man of the Match after an immense 25 tackles and 11 carries – not to mention a disallowed try!

Elliot Daly touched down in the 29th minute, following his own wonderful kick through and then pressure from Jack Nowell. Ireland struck back with a try before half-time, before Henry Slade underlined the difference between the sides with two tries in the last 20 minutes.

Elsewhere Scotland beat Italy, and Wales saw off a strong first-half performance by France to win 24-19.

**Moment of the match:
Return of the Manu!**

10 OUT OF 10. GO STRAIGHT TO THE TOP OF THE CLASS!

England 44-8 France
Twickenham Stadium
10th February 2019

Another thrilling performance gave England a big win over France.

The star of the show was Jonny May. The winger racked up some incredible statistics: scoring three tries in the first 30 minutes (from only four touches of the ball - and all in the same corner as well!) meaning that he had scored 12 tries in 12 matches.

The best of May's tries was his second - receiving the ball standing still and tight against the touchline, May was faced with his opposing winger, Damian Penaud. In the blink of an eye, he dodged left, right and then left again - before crossing the line with ease. Penaud could barely lay a finger on him. World class! Overall it was a magnificent display from England. The team dazzled with speed and power all over the pitch.

Elsewhere Wales beat Italy and Ireland saw off Scotland in a thrilling match at Murrayfield. England were, therefore, top of the table with a maximum 10 points.

Moment of the match: Jonny May's brilliant second try.

CLOSE, BUT NOT CLOSE ENOUGH

Wales 21–13 England
Principality Stadium
23rd February 2019

England could not match the really high standards of the first two matches, and lost to a great Welsh team in Cardiff.

Although England began well, and could have been well ahead by half-time, this was not quite the team who had outclassed France and Ireland. A ferocious Welsh team matched England physically, and never gave Jones' men a second to breathe.

There were bright spots in the England performance – in particular from Tom Curry and Kyle Sinckler. Curry gave the thousands of travelling English fans something to cheer about with a 26th minute try. Sinckler was immense in attack and defence.

Under enormous Welsh pressure, some mistakes began to creep into England's game. The second half belonged to Wales, who scored two tries – with Josh Adams' effort winning the game in the 78th minute.

France beat Scotland, while a below par Ireland defeated Italy in Rome. England were second in the table, behind Wales who now had their eyes set on the Grand Slam.

Moment of the match:
Try by Tom Curry.

EIGHT TRY WONDER.

England 57–14 Italy
Twickenham Stadium
9th March 2019

No match in the Six Nations is ever easy, but this was a routine victory over an Italian side which has never beaten England.

Star of the day was Joe Cokanasiga, who thrilled the Twickenham crowd with his powerful running – often carrying the ball in one hand.

England crossed the Italian line on eight occasions, with Brad Shields scoring

two on his championship debut and Jamie George, George Kruis and Dan Robson each crossing once. Jonny May notched up his fifth try of the season.

Cokanasiga was not the only one showing off some silky skills. Hooker Jamie George threw an incredible long pass for Tuilagi's second try. Kyle Sinckler and Billy Vunipola took the opportunity to show off their kicking skills!

Most importantly, England secured the bonus point win. Wales remained on course for a Grand Slam by beating Scotland, whilst Ireland saw off France. Thanks to their impressive bonus point record, England stood a chance of winning the championship as it entered its final day.

Moment of the match:
Immense pass by Jamie George!

from Tom Curry, Joe Launchbury and Jonny May quickly following.

It could hardly have looked better for England - a 31-0 lead before the half hour mark and the opposition looking tired and well beaten. When Scotland skipper McInally scored after 34 minutes it appeared to be a small blip on the way to an England win.

The second half was a different story: amazing rugby but often difficult for the Twickenham crowd to watch. Scotland scored a further 31 unanswered points to lead 38-31.

As the match entered its final minute England refused to give up. Going for the Scottish line again and again, before finally releasing the ball to Ford who found space to cross under the posts. He converted his own try to secure the draw.

WOW!

England 38-38 Scotland
Twickenham Stadium
16th March 2019

Surely one of the most amazing matches Twickenham has ever seen!

England started well against Scotland with an offensive blitz straight from the kick off. Jack Nowell opened the scoring in the first minute, with tries

Wales won the Grand Slam by beating Ireland and France beat Italy. England finished second in the championship table with 18 points.

Moment of the match: Try by George Ford rescues a draw.

Jonny MAY

Jonny May began to play rugby at the Royal Wootton Bassett club aged five. During his teenage years he faced challenges as other players developed more quickly into bigger, stronger opponents.

He was not discouraged, however, and worked hard at his game. He was eventually taken on by Gloucester, and then England. He now plays for Leicester Tigers.

Jonny was top scorer in the 2019 Six Nations.

Jonny's six tries included a brilliant first half hat-trick against France. His excellent performances throughout the season also meant he was chosen as 'Player of the Year' by his teammates. Quite a year!

A lightning quick winger, Jonny also has incredible agility and the ability to 'smell' a try from nowhere. Trying to mark him is a nightmare for opponents, as no-one knows exactly what he will do next.

TOP TRY

Check out Jonny's debut try, against New Zealand in 2014. Awesome speed!

> **Be positive. Work out what is your best skill, develop it and then believe in yourself during a game.**

JONNY *FACT FILE*
TRUE OR FALSE?

Four of these five facts about Jonny are true, but can you spot the odd one out?

1 Singer Ed Sheeran was a childhood friend of Jonny's.

2 Jonny once came 7th in a national pole vault championship.

3 He had a trial with Swindon Town Football Club.

4 Jonny trained with champion Olympic sprinter Michael Johnson.

5 He once played prop for England.

The answer is on page 60.

HOW WELL DO YOU KNOW ENGLAND'S STAR PLAYERS?

Owen **Farrell**
Harry **Glover**
Jack **Nowell**
Poppy **Cleall**
George **Ford**
Harry **Williams**
Tom **Curry**
Henry **Slade**
Will **Muir**
Ellis **Genge**

Can you match the names of these 10 England stars to the random facts below

BEWARE – there are 10 players but only 9 descriptions. Amazingly, one of the descriptions applies to two of the players!

1 I had a soccer trial for Manchester City and have a twin brother who plays alongside me for Sale Sharks.
Clue: My brother and I are definitely hot stuff on the rugby field.

2 I may be a prop for the Tigers, but my nickname is the Baby Rhino.
Clue: My initials are EG.

3 I went to St George's School, Harpenden and have captained England.

Clue: I can play fly half and I'm a demon kicker...

4 I can't stand tomato ketchup.

Clue: I scored two tries against Ireland in 2019.

5 I love baking, but that's not why I am usually the heaviest player in the England squad!

Clue: I have more hair than most props.

6 I come from a Cornish fishing family and landed a hat-trick on my RWC debut in 2015.

Clue: club side - Exeter Chiefs.

7 My twin sister is also a women's international. I'm a massive fan of Stormzy.

Clue: I may be a Red Rose but my name comes from another flower.

8 I have a first-class degree in Mechanical Engineering. Playing Sevens means a lot of travelling and I love playing computer games to fill in the time.

Clue: You will kick yourself if you get this wrong!

9 I play for England Sevens alongside my younger brother, Will. We both studied at Newcastle University.

Clue: Think winter, cold hands...

Check out the answers on page 60.

Sarah BERN

From spectator to World Cup final and England Player of the Year. The last six years have been quite a journey for Sarah Bern.

Sarah watched from the stands as Sarah Hunter's team won the 2014 Women's Rugby World Cup final in Paris. Three years later she was one of the key players in the Red Roses team which just failed to beat New Zealand in the 2017 final.

You can't have missed Sarah during last year's Women's Six Nations. She was everywhere as England powered to an impressive Grand Slam.

As a prop Sarah was a major part of a pack which often destroyed the opposition scrum. As a former back row forward she was also able to show off her silky running skills – and if that didn't work she could always use her strength to crash through two or three tackles!

The highlight of her season was probably an outrageous try against Wales. She received the ball 20 or 30 yards out, used her pace to break the first defensive line and then deceived the covering players with a perfect sidestep. She finished with an unstoppable drive for the line. Go Sarah!

Sarah is one of the youngest players in the squad. As a student she combined her strength and conditioning course with her England and club careers. In January 2019 she received a full-time playing contract with the RFU.

The **Strange History** of the
RUGBY BALL

There are many jokes made about the shape of a rugby ball. In fact, our great game could not be played with a 'normal' shaped ball.

In rugby the ball is passed or kicked through the air – as opposed to many other games, like soccer, where it is mainly passed along the ground. The egg-like shape of the rugby ball allows it to fly efficiently through the air towards its intended target.

How did the rugby ball end up in its current shape? Well, the story goes all the way back to the 1850s and a man called Richard Lindon.

Lindon made balls for the boys at Rugby School, where the game began. In those days the balls were basically round. They were made from pigs' bladders (which look a bit like balloons) covered in leather.

The shape of the bladder dictated the shape of the ball!

Tragically, Lindon's wife died from an infection caused by blowing into a bladder to inflate the ball. She and Richard had 17 children.

Heartbroken, Lindon decided to find a better way to manufacture the balls. He used rubber for the bladder inside the ball. This was much more flexible than a pig's bladder and allowed the rugby ball to evolve into its distinctive shape.

Who would have thought it?

Egg Fact 1

Eggs have their distinctive shape to keep them safe in the nest. If they were round they could roll out and be smashed.

Egg Fact 2

Rugby balls are not really egg shaped. A rugby ball is symmetrical[1] whereas an egg has one pointed end and one blunt one. Check it out the next time you are in the kitchen!

18

[1]*Symmetrical means a shape is identical on both sides.*

SEVENS

England Sevens teams had a challenging year in 2019 with a lot of ups and downs.

The men's team finished fifth in the HSBC World Sevens Series seeing their best results in Dubai, Sydney and Singapore where they finished in third place each time. Whilst the women's team improved their standing from 2018 by two places to finish sixth.

In July England, as the nominated home nation to represent Team GB, were one of 17 nations contesting the Rugby Europe regional qualifiers for the Tokyo 2020 Olympic Games in France and Russia.

England winning both tournaments, confirmed Great Britain's place in the men's and women's Rugby 7s competitions at the Tokyo 2020 Olympic Games.

Head of England Sevens Simon Amor said: "I'm just so incredibly proud of everyone involved in the programme – men and women. For both teams to qualify GB for the Olympics after the year they've had with huge challenges, huge growth and huge learning is incredible."

England legend James Rodwell retired from playing in 2019 and will become a full-time coach with England.

Making his debut in Dubai in 2008, Rodwell ended his career on a high by scoring his 100th try in his last tournament and series-closing match in Paris.

James Rodwell is the most capped sevens player in history with 91 tournaments, which includes an amazing 69 consecutive appearances. He was part of the Great Britain side that won silver in the 2016 Rio Olympics, a bronze medallist with England in the 2018 Commonwealth Games and holds silver medals from the 2013 and 2018 World Cup 7s.

DID YOU KNOW?

James will become a full time coach with England sevens putting his unique experience and knowledge to good use.

WOMEN'S SIX NATIONS

A TRIUMPHANT SEASON FOR SARAH HUNTER'S WOMEN SAW THEM WIN ENGLAND'S 14TH GRAND SLAM.

England were the first team in the history of the championship to score a perfect 28 points from the five matches. Simon Middleton's team notched up five wins (four points each), five bonus points and a further three points for the Grand Slam.

Middleton was delighted with the season, and especially to see some great young players coming through. All in all, a great step towards the Women's Rugby World Cup in New Zealand in 2021.

Here's a look at how the Grand Slam was won.

Round 1

Ireland 7 – 51 England
Dublin
1st February 2019

A ruthless start to the campaign saw England run in eight tries. Lots of power on display from Sarah Bern. Bryony Cleall scored on her debut.

Round 2

England 41 – 26 France
Castle Park, Doncaster
10th February 2019

This time it was Bryony's twin, Poppy Cleall, who starred – scoring two tries from England's total of seven. England made up for their 2018 defeat by France.

Round 3

Wales 12 – 51 England
Cardiff
24th February 2019

Wales couldn't live with England's power – Sarah Bern was everywhere as England racked up a total of nine tries.

England scored an amazing 45 tries in just 5 matches.

England scored a record 278 points in the championship.

Round 4

England 55 – 0 Italy
Sandy Park, Exeter
9th March 2019

A record crowd of more than 10,000 saw Italy overwhelmed. Nine tries for the Red Roses, including two for winger Jess Breach.

Round 5

England 80 – 0 Scotland
Twickenham Stadium
16th March 2019

HQ saw an awesome display as Scotland were blown away. A total of 12 tries were scored with another two each for Poppy Cleall and Jess Breach.

GEORGE

Jamie is a three-time British Lion, and an impact player of the highest class.

'Jinx' had to wait a long time for a full appearance for England, with his first 18 caps coming as a replacement.

England on their Travels

MURRAYFIELD

This year sees England travel to Murrayfield to play Scotland in the oldest international fixture in rugby.

England have been travelling to Scotland since 1871, and playing at Murrayfield since 1925.

BT Murrayfield is a magnificent, all-seater stadium in the west of the Scottish capital. Now seating 67,800, the stadium's record attendance was an incredible 104,000 for the match against Wales in 1975.

England have traditionally done well at Murrayfield: winning 20 of the 46 games they have played there. Only Lansdowne Road in Ireland has been a more successful away venue.

Let's hope Eddie Jones' men can bring the Calcutta Cup back to Twickenham.

TWICKENHAM VS MURRAYFIELD

Name	Twickenham Stadium	Name	BT Murrayfield
Principal Partner	British Airways	Principal Partner	BT
Location	Twickenham, London	Location	Edinburgh, Scotland
First International	1910	First International	1925
Capacity	82,000	Capacity	67,800

 Come on England!

Martin JOHNSON

Johnson captained England to the title in 2003, with Jonny Wilkinson kicking a last-minute drop goal to defeat Australia in the final.

'Jonno' was a rock-hard lock forward. As captain he turned England into the best team in the world by force of character and determination. Nobody intimidated him and he made sure that the rest of the team followed his example. A real leader.

The 2003 team was coached by Clive Woodward and included great players such as Jonny Wilkinson, Lawrence Dallaglio and Jason Robinson. Other players often captured the headlines but everyone knew that the real heart of the team was Jonno. He was respected throughout the rugby world.

Johnson played for Leicester Tigers throughout his career, winning 307 caps for the club and leading them to four Premiership titles in a row. As well as England, Johnson also played on three tours for the British and Irish Lions.

In total Johnson played 84 times for England, winning an incredible 67 matches. After retiring as a player, he became England Team Manager between 2008 and 2011.

A true England legend.

THE ONLY ENGLAND CAPTAIN TO HAVE LIFTED THE RUGBY WORLD CUP

TWICKENHAM
The Best just got Better!

Twickenham is the biggest rugby stadium in the world. With a stunning new east stand the ground is now better than ever before!

The new east stand is amazing to look at from the outside, putting Twickenham right up with the best stadiums in the world.

The new stand provides an incredible 6,700 square meters of hospitality space.

Sounds big to you? Well, it should do - that's enough space for 100 classrooms! One restaurant alone can seat over 1,000 people for lunch!

Twickenham can hold 82,000 people, making it the second biggest stadium in the UK and the fourth biggest in Europe. The stadium is owned and operated by the RFU, meaning that all profits from ticket sales and hospitality are given straight back to the game.

TWICKENHAM CAN HOLD 82,000 PEOPLE

HERE ARE A FEW FACTS YOU MIGHT NOT KNOW ABOUT THE STADIUM:

Over 200 kilometres of toilet paper are used at a capacity match at the stadium!

The site used to be a market garden, and the ground is sometimes known as the 'cabbage patch'.

The pitch is a mixture of natural and artificial grass. One in every 300 blades of grass (7%) is artificial, helping to give strength and a perfect appearance. Put end-to-end, the artificial grass would stretch around the world.

Some people believe there is a secret tunnel under the pitch, but this is not true.

The stadium is also a top-class concert venue, bands who have played Twickenham include The Rolling Stones, Rihanna and Lady Gaga.

The grass is cut by hand mower – no tractors allowed on the hallowed turf! The ground staff walks more than five miles each time the pitch is cut - to make sure it is in perfect condition.

PLAYER, PITCH, POSITION!

CENTRE
MANU TUILAGI

There are two centres in a rugby team: inside centre (number 12) and outside centre (13). They need to be very powerful, both when running in attack and tackling in defence. They have to communicate well with their teammates.

The number 10 usually accepts the pressure of kicking for goal.

FLY HALF
GEORGE FORD

The fly half wears the number 10 shirt, and is in many ways the most important player in a rugby team. He or she makes crucial decisions all the time: when to run, when to kick, where to attack, who to pass to...

RUGBY IS A GAME FOR EVERYONE AND RUGBY PLAYERS COME IN ALL SHAPES AND SIZES.

Rugby is also a physical game, and can be technical. Whilst every member of the team needs to be fit and to have good ball-handling skills, each position on the field also has its own requirements and attributes. Here's a look at four great players and the skills they need to be world-class in their position:

NO 8
BILLY VUNIPOLA

To be a good No 8 you need to be powerful and very dynamic. They attack from the base of the scrum, especially when looking for tries close to the opponent's line. They are also expected to contribute in attack and defence right across the pitch.

HOOKER
AMY COKAYNE

Another key decision maker in the team. The hooker coordinates the scrum and hooks the ball back to their pack. At the lineout they are expected to give inch perfect ball - even when exhausted sand under extreme pressure.

BEHIND EVERY GREAT PLAYER THERE IS A GREAT TEAM.

BEHIND EVERY GREAT TEAM THERE IS A GREAT ORGANISATION.

England Rugby

The Rugby Football Union (RFU) exists to make sure rugby, and its values, flourish throughout England. It is the oldest and largest rugby union in the world.

2.5 million people play rugby in England, with more than 2,000 clubs and 1,400 schools fielding teams every week. None of this would be possible without the RFU.

The RFU owns and runs Twickenham Stadium

HRH PRINCE HARRY

is the RFU's patron. Queen Elizabeth II was patron for an extraordinary 64 years between 1952 and 2016.

The RFU is responsible for running the great England sides we see playing at Twickenham, but here are a few other facts you might not know about the organisation:

1 All profits made by the RFU are invested in the game, a total of over £100 million in 2018 alone. Incredible!

2 Does your club need new dressing rooms? A better pitch? Floodlights for winter training sessions? Get in touch with your local Rugby Development Officer and apply for a grant from the Rugby Football Foundation – most of the money comes straight from the RFU.

3 The RFU was founded in 1871. Until 1890 it was responsible for defining the rules of rugby for the whole world. That job is now done by World Rugby in Dublin.

4 As well as the senior men's and women's teams the RFU also runs the Under 20s teams, the England Sevens programme and many others.

5 England Deaf rugby is supported by the RFU, they recently beat New Zealand three times.

6 The World Rugby Museum tells the story of rugby around the world. It's based at Twickenham Stadium and is run by (who else..?) the RFU.

7 All Schools launched in 2012 as a Rugby World Cup 2015 Legacy programme, by the end of 2019 750 additional state secondary schools and 1 million children had been introduced to rugby through this initiative.

Mako
VUNIPOLA

Mako Vunipola is possibly the
BEST LOOSE–HEAD PROP IN THE WORLD.

To be an international prop you have to be capable of packing down against a top-class opponent 15 times in a match. You also have to lift an 18-stone lock forward high into the air in the lineout – and repeatedly join rucks and mauls. If you don't make 20 tackles your coach will want to know why.

These are the 'ordinary' tasks of players in Mako's position - and he does them brilliantly. Where he differs from many other props, however, is in what else he can offer.

Mako is a natural runner and carries the ball far more than most props. He has amazing ball-handling skills for a front row forward. He made a superb inside pass to set up a try for Jack Nowell against Scotland in 2016.

If all that wasn't enough, Mako is more than capable of knocking a conversion over from the touchline, or sending a drop-goal clean through the posts!

No wonder the England coaching team consider him to be the complete rugby player. England never look quite the same team when Mako is not playing.

Mako is the elder brother of England No 8 Billy. Both are very proud of their Tongan heritage. Their father Fe'ao represented Tonga in two World Cups, and six uncles and their grandfather also played for Tonga.

The Official RFU
QUIZ

Here's a quiz for all you stats fans. The questions are based on the 2019 Guinness Six Nations. There are questions for everyone – from beginners to the real rugby expert. If you get stuck, you can find many of the answers in this Annual. The answers are on page 60. Good luck!

1 How many players are there in a rugby team?

☐ a. 20 ☐ b. 15 ☐ c. 13

2 How many tries did Jonny May score in the first half against France in the Six Nations?

☐ a. 3 ☐ b. 1 ☐ c. 5

3 Twins Bryony and Poppy Cleall both played for England in the 2019 Six Nations. Which one scored two tries against France?

4 What is the capacity of Twickenham Stadium?

☐ a. 82,000
☐ b. 20,000
☐ c. 200,000

5 Who is the patron of the RFU?

☐ a. Prince Harry
☐ b. President Trump
☐ c. Owen Farrell

6 How many tries did England Women score in their triumphant 2019 Six Nations campaign?

☐ a. 2 ☐ b. 45 ☐ c. 212

7 Which England player was top scorer in the 2019 Six Nations with 59 points?

☐ a. Owen Farrell
☐ b. Mako Vunipola
☐ c. Henry Slade

8 What number does a hooker wear?

☐ a. 3 ☐ b. 15 ☐ c. 2

9 Which side did England <u>not</u> beat in the 2019 championship?

☐ a. Ireland
☐ b. Scotland
☐ c. France

10 Who was voted England's 2019 Player of the Year?

☐ a. Billy Vunipola
☐ b. Jonny May
☐ c. Tom Curry

James
RODWELL

Goodbye to an England Sevens legend! England Sevens' most capped player.

James retired in 2019 after an incredible career and joined the coaching team.

GOOD LUCK JAMES

WOMEN'S

FROM STRENGTH TO STRENGTH

A massively successful national team. Thousands of players. Hundreds of school and club sides around the country. Millions of people watching on TV.

If you want a sporting success story, then look no further than the development of women's and girls' rugby in England.

At the top of the women's game in England are Sarah Hunter's Red Roses. They were World Cup finalists in 2017 and comfortably won the 2019 Six Nations Grand Slam. 28 of the squad are now full-time professionals.

The real success story of the women's game is at the grassroots level with 37,000 women and 60,000 girls playing the game every week, up and down the country.

Rugby is a great sport. It keeps you fit and is a brilliant way of making friends for life. People of any shape or size can play. You learn new skills and develop confidence in yourself.

GRAND SLAM
CHAMPIONS 2019

RUGBY

No wonder female rugby is expanding so fast! Take a look at these amazing facts and figures:

- 25% of all registered rugby players in the world are now female.
- Female players in England doubled in number between 2014 and 2018.
- 10,545 people watched the Red Roses beat Italy at Sandy Park, Exeter in 2018.
- More than 2.5 million people watched the Women's Rugby World Cup Final on TV.
- More than 300 clubs in England have women's teams.
- 137 caps - Rochelle 'Rocky' Clark is the most-capped England international, male or female.
- The RFU made a £2.4 million investment in the Tyrrells Premier 15s in 2017.

Maro
ITOJE

The player who has it all.

Maro is a supremely talented rugby player. Aged only 25, he is already a fixture in the England side.

Maro went to St George's in Harpenden, the same school as his England mates George Ford and Owen Farrell.

WORDSEARCH

Help Ruckley find 24 rugby related words in the maze of letters. Look carefully - they might be vertical, diagonal or even back-to-front! Happy hunting! Answers on page 61.

```
K Y T Z L N I A T P A C D H Z R
J B N Y B V S T L S L N K L C L
R N J R J J T S C M A Y A T W M
L E G T Q C E R E L V N P E R M
R Z F J H C U N G N I N B J W A
D R S E O M V N I F N B G C M H
R Y H E R N E F Q L E I O V Y N
O S L W S E N T L L H A U E N E
P T P V M O E Y L A C C L G V K
G A R L L T R I M H N K U M M C
O D O R L Q S D Q A C K T O L I
A I P H A X L Z E U Y L E Q T W
L U W Y B R K L R R M Y N R P T
L M C L P E N A L T Y M A U L B
Z W M R E K O O H W I N Z N R T
K B T P R T X N I B N I S P F G
```

- Try
- England
- Penalty
- Referee
- Stadium
- Webb Ellis
- Hooker
- Touchline
- Ball
- Final
- Win
- Jonny May
- Drop Goal
- Coach
- Sin Bin
- Guinness
- Twickenham
- Ruckley
- Maul
- Flanker
- Prop
- Scrum
- Captain
- Red Roses

Katy
DALEY–
MCLEAN

Katy was England's captain when they won the Women's Rugby World Cup in 2014.

Since then she has gone on to win over 100 caps and score more than 500 points. Only Owen Farrell and Jonny Wilkinson have scored more in an England shirt!

SPOT THE BALL

Can you help Ruckley find the CORRECT BALL?
Answer on page 61.

2

5

3

1

6

4

Henry SLADE

DO YOU WANT TO KNOW HOW TO PLAY AT OUTSIDE CENTRE?

If so, you should look at Henry Slade's performance against Ireland in the 2019 Guinness Six Nations.

Slade was immense throughout this crucial match. His two tries grabbed the headlines, but they were only part of the story. His passing and kicking were superb.

Henry is not enormous for a modern-day centre, but he was powerful in attack and defence and showed great pace. His second try, from an interception, showed his ability to read the game and his handling skills.

The complete centre!

Henry played for England Under 18s, Under 20s and England Saxons before making his full debut. Throughout his career he has had to manage his diabetes, which was diagnosed when he was 18.

He has type 1 diabetes, which means that his body does not produce sufficient insulin. He has to pay attention to his blood sugar levels, especially when playing and training. During every international, for example, he is quick to leave the pitch at half time. This gives him plenty of time to have his blood tested and then join the other players for the team talk.

Henry is keen for people to know that having diabetes doesn't stop you being a top-class sportsman or woman. In fact, if you look after yourself properly, diabetes doesn't stop you from doing anything.

SLADE FACT 1:
Henry can't stand ketchup!

SLADE FACT 2:
Henry's dog is called Frank and he often goes dog walking with other members of the Exeter Chiefs team (and their dogs!)

2018/19
Match Stats

Included here are the key stats from the 2018 Quilter Internationals, and England's 2019 Six Nations games.

Venue: Twickenham Stadium
Date: 3rd November 2018

🏴 ENGLAND `12`

Tries: -
Con: -
Pen: *Farrell (3), Daly*

🇿🇦 SOUTH AFRICA `11`

Tries: *Nkosi*
Con: -
Pen: *Pollard (2)*

Venue: Twickenham Stadium
Date: 10th November 2018

🏴 ENGLAND `15`

Tries: *Ashton, Hartley*
Con: *Farrell*
Pen: -
Drop: *Farrell*

🇳🇿 NEW ZEALAND `16`

Tries: *McKenzie*
Con: *Barrett*
Pen: *Barrett (2)*
Drop: *Barrett*

Venue: Twickenham Stadium
Date: 17th November 2018

🏴 ENGLAND `35`

Tries: *Care, Wilson, Cokanasiga, Hartley*
Con: *Ford (3)*
Pen: *Daly, Ford (2)*

🇯🇵 JAPAN `15`

Tries: *Nakamura, Leitch*
Con: *Tamura*
Pen: *Tamura*

Venue: Twickenham Stadium
Date: 24th November 2018

🏴 ENGLAND `37`

Tries: *May, Daly, Cokanasiga, Farrell*
Con: *Farrell (4)*
Pen: *Farrell (3)*

🇦🇺 AUSTRALIA `18`

Tries: *Folau (2)*
Con: *Toomua*
Pen: *Toomua (2)*

🇫🇷 IRELAND 20

Tries: *Healy, Cooney*
Con: *Sexton (2)*
Pen: *Sexton (2)*

🏴 ENGLAND 32

Tries: *May, Daly, Slade (2)*
Con: *Farrell (3)*
Pen: *Farrell (2)*

🏴 ENGLAND 44

Tries: *May (3), Slade, Penalty Try, Farrell*
Con: *Farrell (3)*
Pen: *Farrell (2)*

🇫🇷 FRANCE 8

Tries: *Penaud*
Con: *-*
Pen: *Parra*

🏴󠁧󠁢󠁷󠁬󠁳󠁿 WALES 21

Tries: *Hill, Adams*
Con: *Biggar*
Pen: *Anscombe (3)*

🏴 ENGLAND 13

Tries: *Curry*
Con: *Farrell*
Pen: *Farrell (2)*

🏴 ENGLAND 57

Tries: *George, May, Tuilagi (2), Shields (2), Kruis, Robson*
Con: *Farrell (4), Ford (3)*
Pen: *Farrell (1)*

🇮🇹 ITALY 14

Tries: *Allan, Morisi*
Con: Allan (2)
Pen: *-*

🏴 ENGLAND 38

Tries: *Nowell, Curry, Launchbury, May, Ford*
Con: *Farrell (4), Ford*
Pen: *Farrell*

✖ SCOTLAND 38

Tries: *McInally, Graham (2), Bradbury, Russell, Johnson*
Con: Russell (2), Laidlaw (2)
Pen: *-*

England Rugby

MEN'S SEVENS

#TOKYO2020
Qualification Event for the Games of the XXXII Olympiad
in Tokyo in 2020

Qualified

WORLD RUGBY™

WOMEN'S SEVENS

England Rugby

MEN'S

WOMEN'S

England Rugby

Player

PROFILES

Forwards

Ellis GENGE

Club	**Leicester Tigers**
Position	**Prop**
Height	**1.87m**
Weight	**113kg**
Debut	**Wales, 2016**
Caps	**10**
Points	**0**

Jamie GEORGE

Club	**Saracens**
Position	**Hooker**
Height	**1.83m**
Weight	**109kg**
Debut	**France, 2015**
Caps	**37**
Points	**10**

Maro ITOJE

Club	**Saracens**
Position	**Lock**
Height	**1.95m**
Weight	**115kg**
Debut	**Italy, 2016**
Caps	**27**
Points	**5**

Players and statistics correct as of 15 August 2019. England caps and points only.

Dan COLE

Club	**Leicester Tigers**
Position	**Prop**
Height	**1.91m**
Weight	**118kg**
Debut	**Wales, 2010**
Caps	**86**
Points	**20**

Luke COWAN-DICKIE

Club	**Exeter Chiefs**
Position	**Hooker**
Height	**1.84m**
Weight	**112kg**
Debut	**France, 2015**
Caps	**12**
Points	**5**

Tom CURRY

Club	**Sale Sharks**
Position	**Flanker**
Height	**1.85m**
Weight	**99kg**
Debut	**Argentina, 2017**
Caps	**11**
Points	**10**

George KRUIS

Club	**Saracens**
Position	**Lock**
Height	**1.98m**
Weight	**113kg**
Debut	**New Zealand, 2014**
Caps	**33**
Points	**10**

Joe
LAUNCHBURY

Club	**Wasps**
Position	**Lock**
Height	**1.96m**
Weight	**118kg**
Debut	**Fiji, 2012**
Caps	**59**
Points	**25**

Courtney
LAWES

Club	**Northampton Saints**
Position	**Lock**
Height	**2.00m**
Weight	**111**
Debut	**Australia, 2009**
Caps	**72**
Points	**5**

Lewis
LUDLAM

Club	**Northampton Saints**
Position	**Flanker**
Height	**1.88m**
Weight	**98.5**
Debut	**Wales, 2019**
Caps	**1**
Points	**0**

Kyle
SINCKLER

Club	**Harlequins**
Position	**Prop**
Height	**1.83m**
Weight	**113kg**
Debut	**South Africa, 2016**
Caps	**22**
Points	**0**

Jack
SINGLETON

Club	**Saracens**
Position	**Hooker**
Height	**1.80m**
Weight	**108kg**
Debut	**Wales, 2019**
Caps	**1**
Points	**0**

Sam
UNDERHILL

Club	**Bath Rugby**
Position	**Flanker**
Height	**1.86m**
Weight	**103kg**
Debut	**Argentina, 2017**
Caps	**9**
Points	**0**

Players and statistics correct as of 15 August 2019. England caps and points only.

Joe
MARLER

Club	**Harlequins**
Position	**Prop**
Height	**1.84m**
Weight	**110kg**
Debut	**South Africa, 2012**
Caps	**59**
Points	**0**

Mako
VUNIPOLA

Club	**Saracens**
Position	**Prop**
Height	**1.80m**
Weight	**121kg**
Debut	**Fiji, 2012**
Caps	**53**
Points	**5**

Billy
VUNIPOLA

Club	**Saracens**
Position	**No 8**
Height	**1.88m**
Weight	**126kg**
Debut	**Argentina, 2013**
Caps	**42**
Points	**35**

Mark
WILSON

Club	**Newcastle Falcons/ Sale Sharks**
Position	**Flanker**
Height	**1.88m**
Weight	**107kg**
Debut	**Argentina, 2017**
Caps	**13**
Points	**5**

Players and statistics correct as of 15 August 2019. England caps and points only.

55

England Rugby

Player PROFILES

Backs

Owen FARRELL

Club	Saracens
Position	Fly half
Height	1.88m
Weight	92kg
Debut	Scotland, 2012
Caps	70
Points	816

George FORD

Club	Leicester Tigers
Position	Fly half
Height	1.78m
Weight	84kg
Debut	Wales, 2014
Caps	56
Points	260

Piers FRANCIS

Club	Northampton Saints
Position	Centre
Height	1.82m
Weight	92kg
Debut	Argentina, 2017
Caps	5
Points	5

Players and statistics correct as of 15 August 2019. England caps and points only.

Joe
COKANASIGA

Club	**Bath Rugby**
Position	**Wing**
Height	**1.93m**
Weight	**122kg**
Debut	**Japan, 2018**
Caps	**5**
Points	**15**

Elliot
DALY

Club	**Saracens**
Position	**Full-back**
Height	**1.84m**
Weight	**94kg**
Debut	**Ireland, 2016**
Caps	**31**
Points	**79**

Willi
HEINZ

Club	**Gloucester Rugby**
Position	**Scrum half**
Height	**1.81m**
Weight	**90kg**
Debut	**Wales, 2019**
Caps	**1**
Points	**0**

Jonathan
JOSEPH

Club	**Bath Rugby**
Position	**Centre**
Height	**1.83m**
Weight	**90kg**
Debut	**South Africa, 2012**
Caps	**41**
Points	**85**

Jonny
MAY

Club	**Leicester Tigers**
Position	**Wing**
Height	**1.88m**
Weight	**90kg**
Debut	**Argentina, 2013**
Caps	**45**
Points	**120**

Players and statistics correct as of 15 August 2019. England caps and points only.

Ruaridh
MCCONNOCHIE

Club	**Bath Rugby**
Position	**Wing**
Height	**1.89m**
Weight	**91kg**
Debut	-
Caps	**0**
Points	-

Jack
NOWELL

Club	**Exeter Chiefs**
Position	**Wing**
Height	**1.80m**
Weight	**98kg**
Debut	**France, 2014**
Caps	**33**
Points	**65**

Henry
SLADE

Club	**Exeter Chiefs**
Position	**Fly half**
Height	**1.88m**
Weight	**87kg**
Debut	**France, 2015**
Caps	**22**
Points	**25**

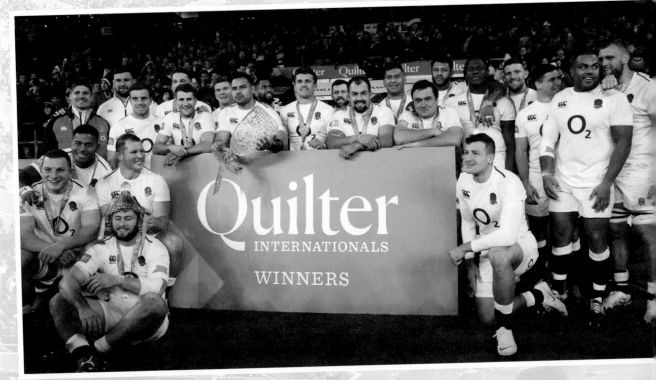

WE ARE THE ROSE

Players and statistics correct as of 15 August 2019. England caps and points only.

Manu
TUILAGI

Club	**Leicester Tigers**
Position	**Centre**
Height	**1.85m**
Weight	**111kg**
Debut	**Wales, 2011**
Caps	**33**
Points	**65**

Anthony
WATSON

Club	**Bath Rugby**
Position	**Full-back**
Height	**1.85m**
Weight	**93kg**
Debut	**New Zealand, 2014**
Caps	**34**
Points	**75**

Ben
YOUNGS

Club	**Leicester Tigers**
Position	**Scrum half**
Height	**1.78m**
Weight	**92kg**
Debut	**Scotland, 2010**
Caps	**86**
Points	**60**

Players and statistics correct as of 15 August 2019. England caps and points only.

JONNY MAY
Page 13

Number 5 is the odd one out.
Playing prop is a specialist position and wingers would not be allowed to play here for safety reasons. However, injuries meant that Jonny was a replacement flanker in a match against Argentina. He was completely confused as to how to bind, and ended up with his head between his prop's legs!

QUIZ
Page 36

1. b. 15.
2. a. 3 – Jonny scored an incredible hat-trick within 30 minutes.
3. Poppy. She scored a total of four tries in the championship, Bryony scored one.
4. a. 82,000.
5. a. Prince Harry.
6. b. 45 – more than any other team in history.
7. a. Owen Farrell.
8. c. 2.
9. b. Scotland – an incredible 38-38 draw. England beat Ireland, France and Italy but lost to Wales.
10. b. Jonny May.

KNOW YOUR ENGLAND STARS
Page 14 and 15

1. Tom Curry
2. Ellis Genge
3. George Ford and Owen Farrell! The two England stars were school friends. Maro Itoje went to the same school.
4. Henry Slade
5. Harry Williams
6. Jack Nowell
7. Poppy Cleall
8. Will Muir
9. Harry Glover

WORD SEARCH

Page 41

SPOT THE BALL

Page 43

Number 3 is the correct ball!

WHERE'S RUCKLEY?

England Rugby   BRITISH AIRWAYS   TISH AIRWAYS

THEM HEAR YOU   #CARRYTHEMHOME   LET THEM HE/